WONDERS OF THE WORLD

GRAND CANYON

Carol Rawlins

Technical Consultant

Stanley S. Beus
Regents Professor
Department of Geology
Northern Arizona University

RSVP

RAINTREE
STECK-VAUGHN
P U B L I S H E R S
The Steck-Vaughn Company

Austin, Texas

A production of B&B Publishing, Inc.

Editor – Jean B. Black
Photo Editor – Margie Benson
Computer Specialist – Katy O'Shea
Interior Design – Scott Davis

Raintree Steck-Vaughn Publishing Staff

Project Editor – Helene Resky
Project Manager – Joyce Spicer

LIBRARY OF CONGRESS CATALOGING-IN-PUBLICATION DATA

Rawlins, Carol.
    The Grand Canyon / by Carol Rawlins
       p. cm. — (Wonders of the world)
    Includes bibliographical references and index.
    ISBN 0-8114-6364-8
       1. Grand Canyon (Ariz.) — Juvenile literature. [1. Grand Canyon (Ariz.)]
I. Title. II. Series.
GB566.G72R39 1995   94-14373
979. 1'32 — dc20   CIP
                                   AC

Cover photo	Title page photo	Table of Contents page photo
Sunrise over the Grand Canyon	North Rim, Cape Final area	Colorado River in the Grand Canyon

PHOTO SOURCES

Cover Photo: Tom Bean

© John Barger: 37, 61
© 1992 Ron W. Bohr Photography: 1, 47 right, 49, 53 right, 54 top, 55
Dave Buchen: 41
Buffalo Bill Historical Center, Cody, WY: 10 right
Bureau of Reclamation, Lower Colorado Region: 28
California Department of Water Resources: 27 both
© Robert Campbell: 22, 47 top, 53 top
Canadian Park Service/Jean Audet: 52 left, 54 middle
Dr. Lloyd Goding: 44, 45 left
Grand Canyon National Park: 8 right, 10 left, 12 both, 13, 14, 52 bottom, 56
© Gary Kramer: 48
© Gary Ladd 1990: 15, 36 bottom, 39, 50
National Park Service photo by Mary O'Brien: 46 bottom

National Park Service photo by Richard Frear: 5, 30 top, 54 bottom
National Park Service photo by William Belknap: 30 bottom
National Park Service/Coronado National Monument: 9
National Park Service: 4, 7, 8 right, 29 both, 32 both
© Greg Probst: 58
Salt River Project: 31
Santa Fe Railway Photography: 45 right
© Eugene Schulz: 3, 6, 8 left, 18, 20, 21, 23, 25, 33, 35, 36 left, 40, 43 both, 46 top, 60 both
Southwest Studies, Maricopa Community College 11
U.S. Fish & Wildlife Service/Debra Bills: 24 both, 26, 51
© Richard Weston: 57, 59

Printed and bound in the United States of America.
    2 3 4 5 6 7 8 9 10 VH 99 98 97 96

Table of Contents

Chapter One

Grand Indeed!

The sun is still below the horizon at the Grand Canyon as an elderly couple halts in their slow descent down Bright Angel Trail. On a ledge nearby, a pair of desert bighorn sheep, timid by nature, stand motionless. It is a thrilling moment for the visitors. Although they come to the canyon regularly, they have not seen the endangered bighorns so close for years. Suddenly the spell is broken. Startled by the sounds of approaching hooves, the sheep silently scamper away. The visitors move aside to let a mule train pass.

The mule riders grin as they go by, grateful that they aren't passing walkers farther down where the trail narrows and the mules must lean way out over the canyon. One nervous rider checks his watch, aware that he has fifteen minutes in which to change his mind about going to the bottom of the canyon. He finds little consolation in the thought that thousands of tourists before him, including Teddy Roosevelt, safely reached the canyon floor on muleback and returned to tell the tale.

At the bottom of the canyon, 5,000 feet (1,500 m) below, whitewater rafters who camped during the night on a small beach beside the Colorado River finish breakfast. They pack up their sleeping gear and trash, including their human waste, knowing that their behavior will help determine whether future rafters will be allowed to float down the river and "run" the rapids. Some of the rapids are rated as "10s," which means that they are among the most dangerous in the world. The rafters also know that, within hours, the level of the river will rise, its volume increased when water is released upriver through Glen Canyon Dam. The experienced guides keep their eyes on the water level, grateful that the timing of the water release is more predictable than it used to be.

Miles across the canyon, on the North Rim, a National Park Service ranger starts down Roaring

Located on the South Rim of the Grand Canyon, Bright Angel Trail drops a mile to the Colorado River at the bottom of the canyon. A few mules have fallen over the side, but no human life has been lost on the trail.

"The Grand Canyon fills me with awe. It is beyond comparison, beyond description; absolutely unparalleled throughout the wide world. Let this great wonder of nature remain as it is now. Do nothing to mar its grandeur, sublimity, and loveliness."
— Theodore Roosevelt in 1903

A lone visitor views the majesty of the Grand Canyon (right).

Springs Trail. The pipe that gathers water at Roaring Springs halfway down the north wall of the canyon is not working properly, and 20,000 thirsty visitors to Grand Canyon National Park will be at the South Rim today. The pipe descends to the bottom of the canyon, crosses 14 miles (22.5 km) of the canyon floor, and climbs up the south canyon wall to the South Rim. The ranger wonders if boulders, loosened during a recent heavy rain, have crashed into the water pipe.

No matter how often or from what vantage point a person experiences the Grand Canyon, each encounter seems new. The senses are always startled. Little in our everyday lives prepares us for the Grand Canyon's phenomenal size and majesty.

The Colorado River has cut a deep gorge for more than 1,000 miles (1,600 km). The Grand Canyon, 277 miles (446 km) long, is the river's deepest and most famous canyon.

Without a doubt, the Grand Canyon is the biggest canyon in the world. It is also the longest (277 miles, or 446 km); the widest (18 miles, or 29 km, in places); and the most difficult to get into, through, or around. And it is one of the deepest (more than a mile [1.6 km] in some places). Visitors will have a better grasp of the canyon's size after walking down one of the trails into the canyon. Even after an hour, the sparkling river at the bottom seems no closer.

The Grand Canyon is spectacularly beautiful. Its walls of many colors, which seem to change as the sun moves across the sky, are formed of layers, or strata, of red, pink, purple, white, and brown rock.

Northwest Arizona is home to more than just the Grand Canyon. Neighboring natural wonders include Zion Canyon, Bryce Canyon, Glen Canyon, Monument Valley, the Canyonlands, Cedar Breaks, Rainbow Bridge, Capitol Reef, Arches, Mesa Verde, the Petrified Forest, Oak Creek Canyon, the Painted Desert, the San Francisco Peaks, and many other unusual and colorful landforms.

More than five million people visit the Grand Canyon each year, including more than two million tourists from other nations. Only one visitor in ten makes the 5-hour, 214-mile (344-km) trip by car around the east end of the canyon to the North Rim.

Most people view the canyon from the relative safety and comfort of a rim. A much smaller number of hikers, mule riders, and white-water rafters see the canyon from deep within its steep walls. Visitors determined to follow a trail to the canyon floor can choose between riding mules and walking. A hardy or experienced hiker can walk a trail 11 miles (17.7 km) down and back up to the other rim.

The Grand Canyon is just one of many natural wonders in a region of geologic marvels. Bryce Canyon National Park is located in southern Utah, not far from the Grand Canyon.

Though thousands have made the trip, it is difficult, especially in summer, when the temperature on the canyon floor is over 100° F (38°C). The steepness of the trails and the heat of the Arizona sun make the trip up twice as long as the trip down. Bright Angel Trail requires four to five hours down for the hiker in average condition and seven to eight hours up. But few who make the trip regret the effort.

Despite its millions of visitors, parts of the Grand Canyon still remain unexplored and uncharted. But that does not mean that humans are something new in Grand Canyon. Native American peoples have lived on the canyon floor and up on the rims for thousands of years. Animal figurines made from split willow twigs as early as 2145 B.C. have been discovered in high caves, as well as many signs of prolonged human habitation, such as trails, fire scars, refuse dumps, granaries, and water-storage hiding places. These signs indicate that early native residents used the canyon like a giant apartment building, moving regularly between the various levels.

Venturing into the Canyon

Captain Garcia López de Cárdenas and his small band of Spanish soldiers were the first Europeans to record seeing the Grand Canyon. In 1540, they were sent by Francisco Vásquez de Coronado, a Spanish officer, to confirm Hopi stories about a "great river flowing in a chasm with walls colored like gold."

Instead of gold, Cárdenas found people living in pueblos, or cliff dwellings, and the spectacular Grand Canyon. When his party arrived on the South Rim, Cárdenas sent three men down to find passage across the river that glinted far below in the bottom of the canyon. On their return, the men, having failed to reach the river, reported the great depth of the canyon and said the river was wider than expected. Cárdenas concluded that the canyon was "worthless" to Spain. It was more than two centuries before another white man recorded a visit to the canyon.

In 1776, Father Francisco Tomás Garcés, having traveled from a mission near Tucson, Arizona,

Native Americans lived on the cliffs of the Grand Canyon and on the river's banks. There may be as many as 50,000 sites. The ruins in the foreground are located by the Kaibab suspension bridge near Phantom Ranch.

Split-twig figurines made of grass or willow twigs were crafted by Native Americans who lived in the Grand Canyon area thousands of years ago. First discovered in Marble Canyon, they were probably good luck charms.

8

climbed down into one of the side canyons of the Grand Canyon. He found a small tribe of Native Americans living there—the Havasupai. Garcés was the first man to consistently refer to the river as the Río Colorado, meaning "red-colored river."

In 1821, control of the region that includes the Grand Canyon was transferred from Spain to Mexico. Twenty-five years later, the United States and Mexico went to war over boundaries and ownership of land, including Texas. The war ended in 1848 with the Treaty of Guadalupe Hidalgo, by which the United States gained the territories of New Mexico and Arizona, including the Grand Canyon region, Texas, and California.

Mormons Settle the North Rim

Members of the Church of Jesus Christ of Latter-day Saints, better known as Mormons, settled the region north of the Grand Canyon in the mid-1800s. Jacob Hamblin, a missionary who came to be called the "Mormon Leatherstocking," led expeditions from southern Utah to the canyon region. He discovered a way to cross the Colorado River near what is known today as Lee's Ferry. He also found another crossing downstream at Grand Wash Cliffs.

Hamblin learned to speak with the Havasupai,

Coronado and other adventurers traveled north along the San Pedro River Valley in Arizona in their search for the land called Quivira and its Seven Cities of Gold. Instead of finding gold, they eventually discovered the Grand Canyon.

Hopi, Paiute, and other tribes of the surrounding plateaus, becoming one of the few white men admired by the Native Americans. He later joined forces with Major John Wesley Powell to explore and chart the northern side of the canyon.

The Mormons and the federal government disagreed about who had authority over the land the Mormons settled. There was frequent conflict between the Mormons and the Native Americans of the region over water and game and the free movement of the tribes over land they considered theirs.

A "Profitless Locality"

Because of continuing friction between the Mormons and the federal government, President James Buchanan sent army troops to Utah in the late 1850s. The army needed a southern route to supply federal troops in Utah and other posts in the West. Charles Christmas Ives of the U.S. Army's Corps of Topographical Engineers was sent to see how far upriver steamships could navigate on the Colorado River.

Ives had a steam-powered stern-wheeler built on the East Coast. It was then taken apart and shipped to the mouth of the Colorado River in Mexico, where it was reassembled. Ives's party traveled 350 miles (564 km) up the Colorado from Fort Yuma in the Arizona Territory to Black Canyon, 78 miles (125.6 km) short of the Grand Canyon. There the boat ran aground on the rocks. Leaving what remained of the stern-wheeler, the party traveled overland to the canyon.

Ives's expedition did little to create interest in the Grand Canyon or in the Colorado River as a cross-country route. Like earlier travelers, Ives concluded: "The region is, of course, altogether valueless. It can be approached only from the south, and after entering it there is nothing to do but leave. Ours has been the first, and will doubtless be the last, party of whites to visit this profitless locality. It seems intended by nature that the Colorado River, along the greater portion of its lonely and majestic way, shall be forever unvisited and undisturbed."

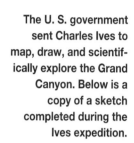

The U. S. government sent Charles Ives to map, draw, and scientifically explore the Grand Canyon. Below is a copy of a sketch completed during the Ives expedition.

Because of the energetic expansion of the Mormons, the North Rim was settled 10 or 20 years before the South Rim. In the 1870s, John W. Young, a son of the Mormon leader Brigham Young, persuaded some English aristocrats to visit the Kaibab, as the North Rim was known. He hoped the Englishmen would consider developing the Kaibab as a sporting area and hunting ground. Buffalo Bill Cody (above) was persuaded by Young to act as guide for the party of 14 from England. The English, however, declined to invest, declaring the area "too far away and too hard to reach."

CAMELS IN THE DESERT

Lt. Edward Fitzgerald "Ned" Beale is shown here disguised as a Mexican. He was sent to survey the region south of the Grand Canyon. This colorful adventurer persuaded the U.S. secretary of war, Jefferson Davis (who would later be president of the Confederacy), to purchase 80 camels for carrying mail, hauling freight, and exploring the desert. However, soon after the camels arrived, all but one of the Arab camel drivers quit, overwhelmed by the canyons, the "fierce" natives, and the desert. American mule drivers never did get the knack of keeping a load on the back of a camel, and the noisy unfamiliar animals stampeded the horses. The camels also were expensive to feed.

With the beginning of the Civil War, Beale's dream was forgotten. The camels were released into the desert where they roamed for years, startling people and livestock. Eventually, all the camels were killed and eaten by hunters when wildlife was scarce.

"An Unknown River to Explore"

After the Civil War, there was considerable interest in the "Arid Region," the name given to the dry uncharted area between the Great Plains and California. The 2,000 square miles (5,150 sq km) in the interior of the Grand Canyon was the largest unexplored section. In 1869, Major John Wesley Powell—a one-armed retired Union officer, college teacher, and amateur naturalist—led a party of ten men in four boats down the Green and Colorado rivers, through Cataract Canyon, Glen Canyon, and, finally, through the 277 miles (446 km) within the Grand Canyon.

As the party entered the Grand Canyon, Powell wrote: "With some feeling of anxiety we enter a new canyon this morning. We have learned to observe closely the texture of the rock. In softer strata we have quiet river, in harder we find rapids and falls. Below us are limestones and hard sandstones which we found in Cataract Canyon. This bodes toil and danger."

Powell was correct. The boats were not suited for the rapids. The men had to carry their boats and supplies around some of the rapids. The trip took much longer than expected, so they were soon running out of food. One man wrote in his diary: "If Major does not do something soon I fear the consequences, but he is content and seems to think that biscuits . . . and a few dried apples is ample to sustain a laboring man."

At the same time, Powell wrote: "We are now ready to start on our way down the Great Unknown. We have but a month's rations remaining. We have

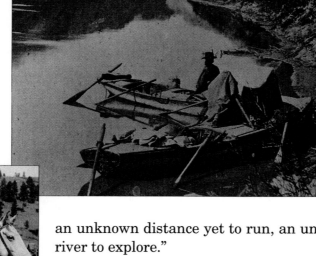

In 1869, John Powell *(below)* and his crew of nine were the first white men to navigate the Colorado River through the Grand Canyon. Powell made a second more extensive expedition in 1871 *(right)*.

an unknown distance yet to run, an unknown river to explore."

Later, the night before three members of the party left the main group, he wrote: "To leave the exploration unfinished, to say that there is a part of the canyon which I cannot explore, having almost nearly accomplished it, is more than I am willing to acknowledge, and I determine to go on."

At a point that came to be known as Separation Rapid, three of the party decided to try and work their way out, discouraged by the shortage of food and fear that the next rapids would mean their deaths. They headed for Mormon villages but were reportedly killed by Native Americans who mistook them for other white men against whom they had grievances.

Powell and his remaining men succeeded in making their way through the canyon on the river. His official report, *The Exploration of the Colorado River of the West,* and his newspaper chronicles informed and excited the American public and, later, the Europeans.

From 1871 to 1872, Powell conducted a second river expedition that was better financed and better equipped. Powell's work as an explorer-scientist opened the West, and he literally put the Grand Canyon and the Colorado River on the map. Thanks to Powell's careful reports and enthusiasm for the Grand Canyon, other explorers, miners, developers, and—eventually—tourists found their way to the Grand Canyon.

Powell's 1877 report concerning land use in the Arid Regions was farsighted, as were his efforts to persuade the National Irrigation Congress to set a good water policy. In 1893, he said to them: "I tell you, gentlemen, you are piling up a heritage of conflict . . . for water rights, for there is not sufficient water to supply the land." Powell was correct. Rights to water are a major issue in every state west of Kansas.

Prospectors and Miners

Prospectors and miners drawn to the canyon played important roles in opening up the Grand Canyon to others. In their search for minerals, they explored the main canyon and the side canyons, named places, and built trails and roads.

In the 1860s, miners had little interest in the plateaus surrounding the canyon. They believed, quite wrongly, that the sedimentary rock that makes up the canyon walls does not contain precious metals. When Powell reported seeing fine gold in the sand of the Colorado River, hundreds of prospectors invaded the area. They found little.

There was a minor gold rush in 1871 in Kanab Canyon on the north side of the Grand Canyon. Later, carbonate of lead, silver, and vanadium were mined in Havasu Canyon, as well as asbestos and copper in the Grand Canyon. But no one got rich. The minerals were too hard to reach and to haul out on burros, and too costly to freight to distant smelters. As the profits from mining waned, the miners and prospectors became guides and hotel operators for the new tourist trade.

Flagstaff, Arizona, a mountain town east of the Grand Canyon, was settled in 1876. Within six years, the transcontinental railroad linked Flagstaff with the East Coast. Train passengers disembarking in Flagstaff still had an uncomfortable wagon ride ahead before they reached the canyon. Nevertheless, the Grand Canyon became more interesting to the traveling public.

On September 17, 1901, the first passenger train reached the Grand Canyon. Travel to the spectacular canyon was cheaper and much faster by rail than by stagecoach.

Railroads to the Canyon

In the late 1880s, S. S. Harper, another prospector, convinced Frank Mason Brown, a Denver real estate man, that a railroad could be built from Grand Junction, Colorado, to Yuma, Arizona. It would then go on to the Pacific by following the Colorado River through the Grand Canyon.

Brown and a party of 14 men set out to complete the survey of the proposed Colorado River railroad. Brown's boat capsized, and his body was never found. Five days later, two other men drowned. A new party completed the survey, but the daring plan for the Denver, Colorado Cañon, and Pacific Railroad was never completed.

The original Bright Angel Hotel was located on the site of the present day Bright Angel Lodge at Grand Canyon Village.

In 1896, Bright Angel Lodge near the head of Bright Angel Trail was established. In 1901, the Santa Fe Railroad constructed a short line called the Grand Canyon Railway to the South Rim from Williams, Arizona. The luxurious El Tovar Hotel was built by Santa Fe four years later and run by Fred Harvey, a famous hotel operator. El Tovar and the Santa Fe made the South Rim a popular tourist attraction.

The Kolb brothers, Ellsworth and Emery, set up a photographic business at the canyon, taking pictures of tourists riding the mules down Bright Angel Trail. They also explored the region, guided geological surveys, lectured, and filmed the river and the canyons for many years.

On the other side of the canyon, the Union Pacific Railroad organized the Utah Parks Company to develop tourist travel in the high plateaus on the north side of the canyon. By 1928, the company had built several rustic lodges—one on the North Rim and others in Zion, Cedar Breaks, and Bryce Canyon parks.

Building a National Park

The United States has been protecting special regions such as the Grand Canyon since 1872. Recognizing that America's "crown jewels" must be protected for the use of all its citizens, the United States was the first nation to establish a system of national parks, national monuments, and recreation areas. Large regions of natural beauty, cultural importance, and recreational interest have been set aside for public use. The legislation that protects America's natural beauty spots controls homesteading, mining, hunting, and other endeavors that benefit only a few Americans.

The rafter on the Colorado River deep within the inner canyon and the airplane passenger flying over it can see that the Grand Canyon is a single, unbroken unit. It begins at Lee's Ferry at the eastern end and goes to the western Grand Wash Cliffs. However, despite the unity of the canyon's geology, the Grand Canyon National Park was assembled bit by bit over a period of 67 years.

U.S. National Park Service officials administer Grand Canyon National Park under orders that require them to "conserve the scenery and the natural and historic objects and the wildlife therein and to provide for the enjoyment of same in such a manner and by such means as will leave them unimpaired for the enjoyment of future generations."

Lee's Ferry, located 13 miles below the Glen Canyon Dam, is the starting point for Colorado River rafters. Here at the beginning of the canyon, steep rock walls are absent.

Some people have continued to try to use the canyon for their own purposes, but eventually, the vastness of the canyon discouraged most of them. The enormous size of the canyon, the very thing that attracted those who came to see and conquer, protected it.

In recent years, however, people have altered life within the Grand Canyon in significant ways. The greatest changes have come about from channeling the Colorado River through Glen Canyon Dam, upriver from the Grand Canyon. Changing the river in the bottom of the canyon is not unlike changing

Jurisdictions in the Grand Canyon Region

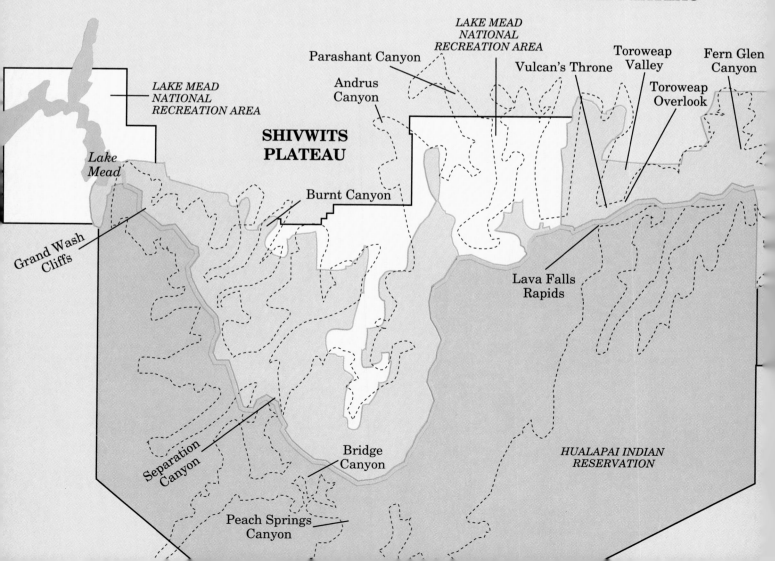

    Grand Canyon National Park Limits

------ Grand Canyon Rim Outline

KANAB PLATEAU

LAKE MEAD NATIONAL RECREATION AREA

Parashant Canyon

Andrus Canyon

Vulcan's Throne

Toroweap Valley

Fern Glen Canyon

Toroweap Overlook

LAKE MEAD NATIONAL RECREATION AREA

SHIVWITS PLATEAU

Lake Mead

Burnt Canyon

Grand Wash Cliffs

Lava Falls Rapids

Separation Canyon

Bridge Canyon

HUALAPAI INDIAN RESERVATION

Peach Springs Canyon

the bloodstream of a living organism. There are some benefits, but there are also dangers.

Environmentalists, naturalists, and anthropologists who are interested in the canyon's ancient ruins, as well as river and wildlife enthusiasts and many others, are alarmed about the Grand Canyon. Conservation, preservation, enjoyment, and the future of the Grand Canyon are increasingly at risk, despite the best efforts of the National Park Service. To understand the risk, we will look at the complexity of the canyon in the next chapters.

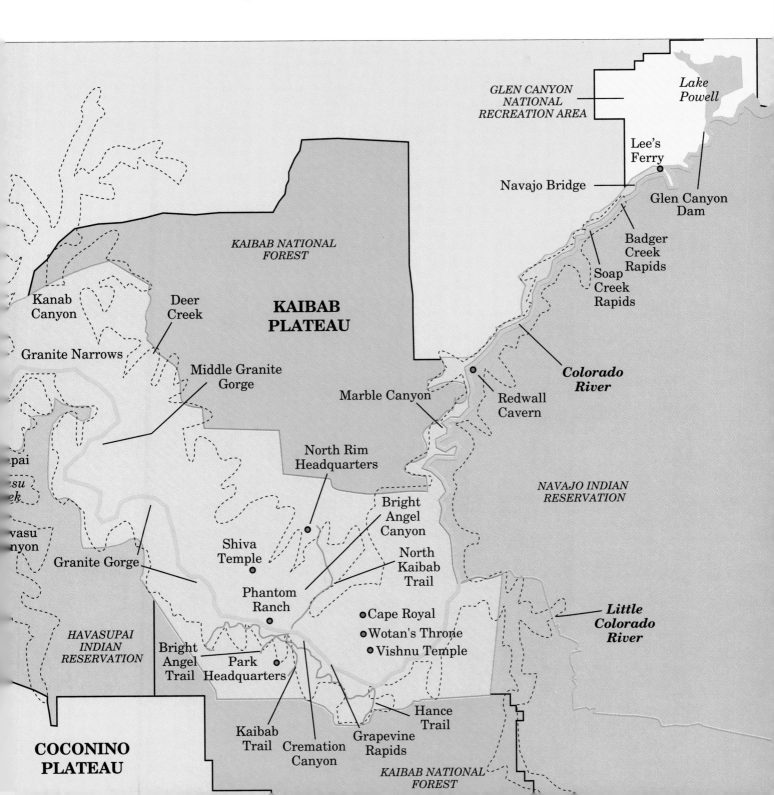

Chapter Two

Water vs. Rocks

Local Native Americans tell stories about the origin of the Colorado River and the people who inhabit the Grand Canyon. The Navajo, Hualapai (also written Walapai), and Havasupai believe the Colorado River is the runoff from a great flood that once covered the Earth. The Hopi also tell of the Big Water and how their people emerged into this world from the underworld through an opening they believe to be deep within the gorge of the Little Colorado River not far from the Grand Canyon. The Navajo also tell similar emergence stories, saying they appeared through a spot near the San Juan River in the Colorado Rockies.

Afternoon thunderstorms are common on both rims of the Grand Canyon in the summer.

The Colorado Plateau

Geologists have another version of the origin of the Grand Canyon. They base their account on evidence revealed in the land surrounding the canyon, as well as by the walls of the canyon itself.

Geologists divide the United States into a dozen or so regions called provinces. These provinces are characterized by similar geological features common to all the territory included within each region.

The Grand Canyon is in the Colorado Plateau Province, which is a 130,000-square-mile (337,134-sq-km) irregular landmass in the Four Corners region of the Southwest, where the four states of Colorado, New Mexico, Arizona, and Utah come together. The plateau is constructed of horizontal layers of sedimentary rock—rock formed from materials that settled out of the ancient seas that once covered the region.

Approximately 65 million years ago, a series of upheavals caused by forces deep within the Earth lifted the land known today as the Colorado Plateau until it had risen several miles. That major upward movement, called upwarping, was followed by millions of years of erosion, or wearing away, of those mountains. Evidence of that eruption can be seen today in ancient rock that has been exposed along the plateau's southern border in New Mexico and Arizona and in the Rocky Mountains of Colorado.

Five million years ago, new rumblings from deep within the Colorado Plateau itself produced another smaller uplift. This action may have started the process of rapid erosion that left a smaller plateau, called the Kaibab Plateau, standing up from the Colorado Plateau. *Kaibab* is a Paiute word meaning "Mountain Lying Down." As the Kaibab Plateau lifted up, it tilted slightly toward the south, so that the top layer of the northern side of the

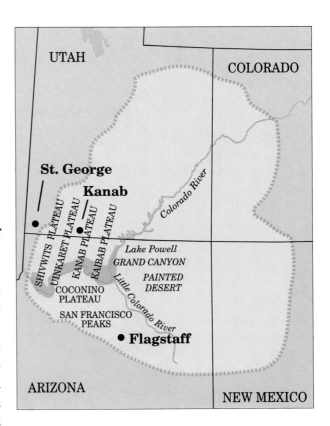

The Colorado Plateau Province (*outlined above*) covers a large area of New Mexico, Arizona, Utah, and Colorado. The Grand Canyon and many smaller but similar plateau formations are found within this region.

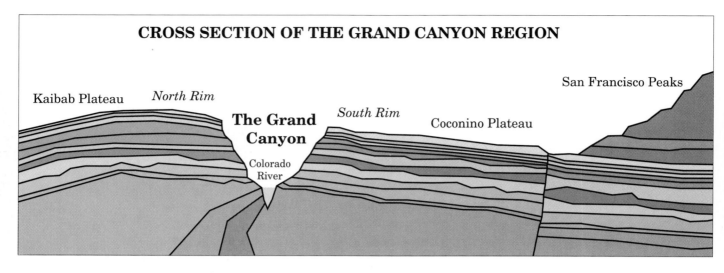

CROSS SECTION OF THE GRAND CANYON REGION

Kaibab Plateau — *North Rim* — **The Grand Canyon** — Colorado River — *South Rim* — Coconino Plateau — San Francisco Peaks

Kaibab Plateau is 1,200 feet (360 m) higher than the top layer of the southern side. The North Rim also tilts toward the canyon, so that water runs off, eroding more and more of the north side. On the South Rim, water runs away from the canyon, so the canyon walls do not erode as much.

The next major geological event in the region took place several million years ago when the Colorado River began to split the Kaibab Plateau into two distinct landmasses. Over time, the river dug out the magnificent series of canyons that distinguish the Colorado Plateau Province.

Geologists discovered that the two sides of the plateau were once connected by studying the walls of the Grand Canyon on both sides of the river. Though separated by the vast empty space of the canyon, the distinctive layers match perfectly. However, even though the two rock masses are part of the same plateau, they are called different names. The land on the north side of the river is called the Kaibab Plateau, while the land south of the river is known as the Coconino Plateau.

The Colorado River separated the Kaibab Plateau from the Coconino Plateau several million years ago. The river slices through Marble Canyon in the picture below.

Water in Motion

Visitors to the Grand Canyon sometimes find it difficult to believe that something so simple and apparently harmless as water could cut a hole as large as the Grand Canyon in the Earth's surface. However, water in motion is one of nature's most powerful ways of altering a landscape.

Water that is not trapped within a lake is pulled downhill toward sea level by the force of gravity. As a trickle of water flows over the ground, it picks up tiny bits of dirt, rock, and sand. In a process geologists call transport, the water carries all those little fragments of soil and rock along. Whether blunt or sharp, like sandpaper or a dentist's drill, the broken-off fragments and debris cut into the surface of the Earth's crust.

The power of water to gnaw away, or erode, the land varies with the slope of the streambed. Streams with greater slope move faster and carry more eroding silt. In a slower, more level stream, silt and sand sink to the bottom, and the water loses its cutting power. The Colorado River originates high in the mountains, descends rather steeply in some places, and carries a heavy load of silt. These facts make the river an amazingly effective carver of canyons.

Lava Falls Rapids are among the most famous rapids in the Grand Canyon.

How to Make a Canyon

Several theories exist as to how the river actually cut a channel through the rock of the Kaibab Plateau. The river-pirating theory holds that at one time the ancestral upper Colorado River flowed southwestward from the Rocky Mountains until it was halted by the Kaibab Plateau. There the river turned southeast toward the Rio Grande, at one point flowing into a huge lake that is now extinct.

Meanwhile, on the western side of the Kaibab Plateau, snow and rain falling on the plateau drained into the Haulapai River, an ancestral river that flowed toward the west. In a process called headward erosion, the water flowing into the Hualapai eroded the head of the valley backward through the rocky region it was draining.

Eventually, the headwaters of the Hualapai wore a channel through the plateau and linked up with the channel of the ancestral upper Colorado River. The lower river "stole" the water from the upper—like a pirate—and thus the two rivers became one. The new river changed course, moving toward the west before it turned south to drain into the Gulf of California.

From that time on, the Colorado flowed from the Rocky Mountains in its original channel as far as the Kaibab Plateau. There, the river slipped into the channel of what had been the Hualapai River,

Over a long period of time, running water carved the Grand Canyon through the process of erosion.

5 million years ago

4 to 5 million years ago

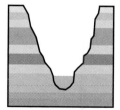

4 million years ago

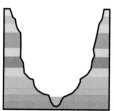

1 million years ago to present

21

Snow blankets the
Grand Canyon in winter
(left). Cracks in the rock
layers are made larger
by snow and ice,
further eroding the
canyon walls and creat-
ing new formations.

changed its course, and flowed on into the Gulf of California.

Another theory holds that the Colorado River already ran through the region before the last uplift of the high plateau. It drained somewhere to the west until the Gulf of California opened up about six million years ago. According to both theories, the upward movement of the plateau was so slow that the river remained near the same elevation by cutting a channel through the plateau as the plateau moved upward. To picture how such a process might work, imagine cutting a cake by holding the knife stationary as you lift the cake upward.

Why the Canyon Is So Wide

Whichever process directed the Colorado through the Kaibab Plateau, the actual work of cutting through the rock was accomplished by transport and erosion. The water carried away the silt and debris left by the eroding action. However, a river will carve only its riverbed, and the Grand Canyon reaches 18 miles (29 km) wide in some places. What happened?

The answer is more erosion—some swift, some slow. The Colorado Plateau is an arid land. With 10 inches (25 cm) or less of precipitation each year, much of the province qualifies as

Rainfall is scarce on the Colorado Plateau. A field of prickly pear cacti survives on the arid land above the Colorado River.

desert. Precipitation in this area occurs mostly in two seasons—summer monsoons and winter snows.

Water does not easily soak into dry land. Instead, it collects in low places until it overflows and rushes downhill as a powerful surge or flood. When this happens, the water carries rock and sand with it. Also, side streams or creeks within the canyon periodically swell with water. Large amounts of debris—including huge boulders—crash downstream, carried by fast currents. The silt- and rock-carrying water rushes into the open spaces of the canyon, wearing away more rock. This weathering, plus landslides, rock falls, and the downhill

creep of loose debris gradually widened the canyon far beyond the width of the river itself.

The Canyon is Growing

Surprisingly, the canyon is still growing. Even the buttes—the flat-topped mountains that rise abruptly from the canyon floor—are wearing away by various processes. Erosion of the rock by weathering—wind, frost, snow, and rain—is responsible.

Geologists know that an additional 4,000 to 6,000 feet (1,200 to 1,800 m) of rock once extended above the current cap layer of the canyon walls. The missing layers were formed of sedimentary rock—rock formed from hardened silt, such as sandstone, limestone, and shale—which was carried away by water, bit by bit, over the centuries.

The canyon walls are further weathered by the twin processes of expansion and contraction. Rain and melting snow sink into the soil or catch in pockets in the rocks. When that water freezes, it expands, widening the cracks in the rocks, and further loosening pieces of rock.

In addition to the temperature changes that expand and contract the rocks as the seasons change, temperature variations within a single day

Named for a botanist, Vasey's Paradise tumbles out of the Redwall limestone in Marble Canyon. Some of the canyon's waterfalls may eventually carve side canyons.

The Grand Canyon has many side canyons accessible from the river. Torrents of water pour from these canyons during spring thaw or after rainstorms.

are great enough to contribute to this weathering. Daytime heat followed by nighttime cold set up a pattern of contraction and expansion that breaks up rocks.

Water also gets help from an unusual source—a plant. Lichens, small, feathery, mosslike plants, have the ability to grow on limestone. The plant produces an acid that breaks down the limestone into soil. Even the smallest pocket of soil can catch seeds dropped by wind and birds. When moisture and sun start the seeds growing, tiny plant roots emerge and work their way into crevices in the rocks. Pieces of rock, dislodged by the roots, fall into the canyon, to be carried away by the side streams and the river.

Rocks gradually weather into soil, or fall, one at a time, into the canyon, further wearing away the surface over which they tumble. Evidence of this process can be seen in the talus—the rocky debris piled up along the banks of the river.

And so the process goes on, year after year, century after century. In a few million years, there will be no Grand Canyon to visit. Instead, the river and the weather will have worked through the plateau, creating a wide river valley where the Grand Canyon once stood.

Sometimes called "the big, pushy river" by guides, the Colorado River alternates between calm water and churning rapids. This constant motion carries rocks and soil that continually change the canyon.

Before the Glen Canyon Dam was operational, the Colorado River carried about 380,000 tons of sediment in its waters every day as it flowed through the Grand Canyon. Today, it carries about 40,000 tons per day.

Chapter Three

The River at the Bottom of the Canyon

"Too thick to drink and too thin to plow."
— **John Wesley Powell of the Colorado River**

For millions of years the vigorous Colorado River flowed freely across the Colorado Plateau. Brick-red, rough and tough, the river cut into the rocky plateau. Its grinding action eventually produced the Grand Canyon and 18 other deep-sided canyons.

The Colorado River begins 14,000 feet (4,200 km) above sea level, in the rain and melting snow of the central Rocky Mountains of Colorado. To reach sea level from that great height, the Colorado must drop nearly 3 miles (4 km).

The Colorado River flows within the boundaries of the Grand Canyon for just 277 miles (446 km) of its 1,450-mile (2,330-km) length. Within that distance, the river drops 1,900 feet (570 m), more than the height of the Empire State Building. Some of the river's downhill movement is gradual and easy, and some is sudden and abrupt, through rapids that are among the most treacherous in the world.

Many rivers, such as the slow-moving Mississippi, are useful for commerce and travel. However, the waters of the Colorado are too turbulent to carry freight or passengers—other than those seeking the thrill of "running" the rapids. The river's drop in elevation is too great for boats larger than rafts to navigate safely. Within the canyon, the river's banks are too steep for boats to dock or freight to be loaded. Also, the river's depth and width are irregular, and its sands may shift.

Father Garcés gave the river the name Río Colorado, Spanish words meaning "red-colored river" because of the brick-red color of its water. The reddish-brown color comes from silt—bits of earth, sand, pebbles, and other debris the river picks up on its long journey from the mountains to Mexico. The Colorado, one of the most silt-filled of North American rivers, has carried away every pebble, boulder, grain of sand, and bit of soil that once filled the Grand Canyon. On an average day before 1963, when Glen Canyon Dam began operation, 380,000 tons of sediment were transported past a measuring point near Phantom Ranch. Periods of flooding increased the weight of the sediment-laden water greatly. The tonnage was so great because the river carries huge boulders in its debris—boulders that are 5 to 14 feet (1.5 to 4 m) in diameter, weighing nearly 50 tons each. Now, since the flow is controlled, 40,000 tons per day is the average.

Claiming the Water

The Colorado River is vital to the 25 million people in the Southwest as a primary source of hydro-electric power and water. The river provides water for agricultural and ranching industries that feed much of the United States. Without the river, the flourishing Southwest would still be empty, semiarid land.

The seventh longest river of the United States, the Colorado and its tributaries travel through seven states—Colorado, Utah, Wyoming, New Mexico, Arizona, Nevada, and California—before flowing into the Gulf of California, in Mexico. All seven states, plus Mexico, claim a share of the water.

In 1922, an agreement called the Colorado River Compact was signed. It decreed how much water each of the seven member states could use. For years, the Upper Compact States—Colorado, Utah, Wyoming, and New Mexico—did not use their full allotment.

California's arid Central Valley has become productive through irrigation water supplied by the Colorado River.

Large aqueducts carry water from the Colorado River to the farming and urban centers of Southern California.

They sold their unused water to the Lower Compact States—Nevada, Arizona, and California. Today, growing populations and agriculture make control of the river a matter of vital interest. Cities, states, ranchers, farmers, Native Americans, and others are locked in dispute and legal action for control of this vital resource.

In 1944, an agreement between the United States and Mexico guaranteed that Mexico's claim for water would be met. Currently, much of the Colorado's water is diverted before the river flows into Mexico. The once full-flowing river is now a small trickle by the time it gets to Mexico. Unresolved questions of rights to the water have created tension between the two nations.

Today, the river is restricted, controlled, and diverted along its route by more than forty dams and diversions. The Colorado River has been called "the most restricted, most legislated" river in the world.

Two Dams

Two major dams, like giant bookends at each end of the Grand Canyon, control the Colorado River as it flows into, through, and out of the Grand Canyon. Hoover Dam is downriver from the Grand Canyon on its westernmost boundary. Glen Canyon Dam is found upriver from the Grand Canyon, outside its eastern border.

Hoover Dam stretches across the Black Canyon of the Colorado River at the Nevada-Arizona border. Lake Mead, created by the dam, is one of the Southwest's most popular recreation areas.

Hoover Dam, originally called Boulder Dam, was built to control flooding and provide hydroelectric power to urban areas. When the dam opened in 1936, it was hailed as one of the country's greatest building achievements. Plenty of water and the seemingly unlimited electrical power produced by channeling the Colorado River through the turbines and generators of Hoover Dam changed Las Vegas from a sleepy desert town to one of the fastest-growing cities in the United States.

Behind Hoover Dam, the Colorado backs up to form Lake Mead, which has become a popular recreation area. It extends into the western edge of the Grand Canyon.

Early visitors to Hoover Dam, Lake Mead, and Las Vegas spread the word that here was a land where the sun always shines and recreation is unlimited. Migration to the Southwest began with a trickle of people but continues today in such large numbers that the region's natural resources, particularly water, are stretched to a critical point.

Glen Canyon Dam, upriver from the Grand Canyon and outside its eastern border, opened in 1964. The dam was intended to guarantee delivery of water from the Upper Compact States to the Lower Compact States, provide flood control, store water, enhance the environment and recreation, and produce hydroelectric power. Glen Canyon Dam was also expected to extend the life of Hoover Dam by catching the silt carried by the Colorado River before it reached, and further damaged, the turbines of Hoover Dam.

Glen Canyon Dam is one of the highest dams in the world. It was built so that the states of New Mexico, Wyoming, Colorado, and Utah could store their portion of Colorado River water.

Lake Powell, created by the water of the Colorado River, extends 186 miles (298 km) behind Glen Canyon Dam's concrete walls.

Lake Powell formed behind Glen Canyon Dam as the water of the Colorado River backed up into Glen Canyon, which is now underwater. Lake Powell is a very large—250 square miles (648 sq km)—and very popular recreation area, drawing perhaps a million visitors each year. Daniel J. Lenihan, an anthropologist and diver who has searched for Native American sites deep in Lake Powell, wrote in *Natural History* magazine that the

The waters of the Colorado River are naturally brownish-red due to the silt and sediment it carries *(right)*. Since the Glen Canyon Dam was built, however, water emerging from the dam is a bluish-green *(top)* because sediment is left behind at the bottom of Lake Powell.

"raging river, a piece of raw wilderness, has been molded into a huge pond."

Environmentalists, naturalists, white-water rafters, and many others are alarmed by the unexpected results of building the dam. Species of fish, mammals, birds, and vegetation that had evolved over millions of years in the Grand Canyon depended on an unrestricted flow of the river. Altering the river by building the dam brought about changes in their habitats that are harming the wildlife.

Among the changes was the temperature of the river water. When flowing naturally, the river water was heated by the sun. Now, the water released through the dam comes from the bottom of deep Lake Powell, where the warmth of the sun never reaches. Some species that depend on seasonal warming of the river have become extinct because of these temperature changes.

Before the dam was built, the river's volume and speed changed with the seasons. Mountain snows would melt in the spring, and summer rains made their way into the river. During other seasons, the flow was leisurely, and the level was low. Today, the water from the mountains collects in Lake Powell and is released through the dam and into the river in periodic surges throughout the day year-round, as power needs rise and fall.

One environmentalist compared these periodic surges to bulldozers plowing through the Grand

Canyon several times each day. Wildlife suffers, boaters are stranded, and prehistoric Indian ruins along the river are washed away.

Another consequence of diverting the Colorado River through Glen Canyon Dam has been that the Colorado's natural load of silt or sediment now sinks to the bottom as its waters slow and form Lake Powell. With its silt gone, the water emerging from Glen Canyon Dam is now blue-green rather than its natural brownish-red. Before the dam, the nutrient-rich silt that now drops into the bottom of Lake Powell was delivered downstream by the current of the river. The river dropped off its silty load as it flowed along, replenishing the land along its banks, including the beaches in the Grand Canyon. The river delivered the rich material it picked up along its 1,450-mile (2,333-km) route as far as its mouth in Mexico. The nutrients that once nourished the land in seven states and Mexico are now trapped behind Glen Canyon Dam.

The pressure of the silt building up behind Glen Canyon Dam leads some experts to estimate the life of the dam at fewer than 200 years. And no one knows what would happen to the silt and water should the dam break.

The Coal Haze

The growing population within the Southwest has continued to increase the demand for more electricity. Water engineers decided in the 1970s that another dam downstream from Glen Canyon Dam was needed. Marble Canyon, which is below Glen Canyon Dam, was the proposed site for the new dam.

Instead of a hydroelectric dam across Marble Canyon, the Navajo Generating Station was constructed near Page, Arizona, in the 1970s. This coal-burning power plant uses up to 1,000 tons of coal per hour.

Environmentalists, upset that they had not stepped in early enough to prevent the construction of Glen Canyon Dam, succeeded in building public opposition that halted the construction of this new dam.

As a compromise, Navajo Generating Station, a coal-fired plant that uses steam to turn the turbines of electrical generators, was built near Page, Arizona. Soon, however, Grand Canyon was facing a new environmental problem. A smoky haze periodically formed over the canyon. It altered the colors of the rocks and prevented visitors from seeing to the far rim. The haze was traced to particles given off by the smokestacks of the Navajo power plant, which was spewing 13 tons (11.8 metric tons) of unfiltered sulfur dioxide into the air every hour.

The 1977 Clean Air Act guarantees clean air in national parks, so the National Park Service filed suit to have devices called scrubbers put on the exhaust towers of the power plant that would remove the haze-making particles. It has now been agreed that by 1999 the sulfur dioxide given off by the generating plant will be reduced 90 percent.

The Navajo power plant is not the only source of haze, however. In summertime, haze mars the view from one rim of the canyon to the other and from the North Rim to the colorful land formations found near the canyon. Apparently, summer air currents are carrying smog from Arizona's urban areas of Phoenix and Tucson and from the California cities of San Diego and Los Angeles. Unfortunately, this haze originates outside the jurisdiction of the National Park Service, so such seasonal pollution will be difficult to stop.

Visibility can be poor at the Grand Canyon due to air pollution, especially in the summer months *(right)*. This haze not only irritates visitors unable to see the beauty of the canyon *(below)*, but it also causes damage to the rock layers.

Chapter Four

A Geologist's Dream

The walls of the Grand Canyon are a perfect classroom for geologists and other people interested in a clear record of the Earth's development. In the 6,250 feet (1,875 m) from the rim to the bottom of the canyon, 2 billion years of geological history are exposed.

Each colorful layer in the canyon walls gives clues to the environment in which that particular stratum, or layer, formed. At various times in its history, the region was covered with ancient seas. As each sea receded, it was replaced by another. At intervals, and to varying degrees, the land dried out. Sometimes the surface was covered with sand; other times, with swamps and small lakes. Earthquakes and volcanoes, dinosaurs and tiny crabs are all part of the region's history.

When standing at the rim of the Grand Canyon, the layer of rock directly under your feet is considered by geologists to be the most recently formed. The thick canyon walls developed from the bottom up—the oldest first, then on up through time until the cap layer formed. Actually, other layers were stacked above the one on which we stand, but they were eroded over time. The oldest rocky formations, which lie in the Inner Gorge in the bottom of the

"One might imagine that this was intended for the library of the gods; and so it was. The shelves are not for books, but form the stony leaves of one great book. He who would read the language of the universe may dig out letters here and there, and with them spell words, and read, in a slow and imperfect way, but still so as to understand a little, the story of creation."

— John Wesley Powell of the Grand Canyon

33

canyon, can best be viewed at eye level from a raft drifting along the Colorado River.

While you read the history of the region as it is revealed in the rock layers, remember that the Grand Canyon itself did not exist at that time. When seas flooded the region, marine fish could not hide in the side canyons to escape predators. Dinosaurs could not unexpectedly fall after a misstep on the rim. The land rose and fell with the Earth's convulsions. Sometimes mountains rose in one part while an ancient sea covered another part. But there was not yet a Grand Canyon.

The Land Before Time

The calendar of events in the Earth's history is called the geologic time scale. The major divisions of the time scale are called eras. The longest era—from the time the Earth's crust formed about 4.5 billion years ago to about 570 million years ago—is called the Precambrian Era. About two billion years ago, during the Precambrian Era, an ancient sea covered the entire Grand Canyon region.

Silt, clay, sand, and mud were dumped into the sea by rivers draining the nearby land. Lava and volcanic ash from erupting volcanoes added to the material building up on the seafloor until the deposit was 5 miles (8 km) deep.

Sediment is the material that sinks to the bottom of a body of water. As more material piles up, the weight of the upper sediment forces the lower sediment to compact. Minerals left by water seeping through the debris then bind the particles together, and the end result of this compacting process is sedimentary rock. Sedimentary rock tends to form horizontal layers.

Sedimentary rock is one of three classes into which geologists divide all rocks. Fossils—the remains of once-living organisms—occur within lay-

---

GEOLOGIC ERAS

Precambrian Era
- 4.5 billion years ago to about 570 million years ago
- Rock types present: shales, siltstones, lava, volcanic ash, and metamorphic rocks
- The Grand Canyon area was underwater.

Paleozoic Era
- About 570 million years ago to 225 million years ago
- Rock types present: limestones, shales, and sandstones
- The Grand Canyon area was underwater.

Mesozoic Era
- 225 million years ago to 65 million years ago
- Rock types present: shales, sandstones, limestones, and chalk
- The Grand Canyon area was above water for the first time at the end of this era.

Cenozoic Era
- 65 million years ago to present
- Rock types included: clays, limestones, and sands
- The Grand Canyon area was repeatedly covered with lava and then carved by erosion during this era, leading to the present-day look of the canyon.

ers of sedimentary rock. Fossils are basic to the study of Earth's history because their presence in rock tells us how long ago the rock was formed. Dealing with millions of years is not always easy, however, and in the following description of the layers, there is still a lot of debate among geologists about just what happened so long ago.

The Dark at the Bottom

The sediment deposited in that early sea compacted into sedimentary rock called shale and sandstone. These layers sank deep into the Earth until they were 10 miles (16 km) or more below the surface.

Then, about 1.7 billion years ago, this sunken shale was uplifted into a mountain range by violent forces within the planet. As the mountains rose, the buried layers buckled and folded. Intense heat and pressure changed the rocks.

Rock that is transformed or altered by intense heat and pressure into a different physical form is called metamorphic rock—the second of three main kinds of rock. The metamorphic rock that resulted from such powerful changes within the Earth formed the shiny, dark rock visible at the bottom of the Inner Gorge. Called Vishnu schist, it is the oldest rock formation of the Grand Canyon. Fossils are rare in these rocks, though evidence of algae, the simplest form of plant life, is found in the Vishnu schist.

The dark bedrock that makes up the walls of Granite Gorge are Vishnu schist and Zoroaster granite, remnants of ancient sedimentary and volcanic activity.

While the rock was still inside the Earth, molten rock, called magma, worked its way into openings in the schist, becoming a different kind of rock, as it cooled, called Zoroaster granite. In many places, the granite forms pinkish, oddly shaped streaks through the black schist. Some granite and shale metamorphosed into gneiss, which can be identified by thin flakes that you can flick off with your thumbnail. Mica is a common example of gneiss.

The mountains that were formed about 1.7 billion years ago gradually eroded away, leaving a flat plain. Other sediments were carried into channels that streams had cut across the surface of the flat plain. For 500 million years, no new stratum of rock was laid down. Periods when regions are being eroded rather than receiving new sediments are called unconformities.

The Supergroup

At the end of the 500 million-year period, things again changed. About 1.2 billion years ago, the region was once more covered with a sea. The water retreated and returned many times. Evidence of this can be seen in the next group of rock layers to form—the Grand Canyon Supergroup. Ripple marks, raindrop impressions, and mud cracks in the rocks of the Supergroup indicate that water did not cover the region at all times.

Water was not the only thing affecting the rock at that time. Volcanoes erupted on the bottom of the sea, and more magma—molten rock inside the Earth—intruded into the rocks. Later, other volcanic eruptions spewed lava and ash onto the land. The rocks in these layers show evidence that seas came and went after the eruptions of the volcanoes.

Eight layers of sedimentary rock were laid down during this period. These eight layers, the Grand Canyon Supergroup, show clearly against the lower canyon wall because they are tilted. The tilting occurred when another upward thrust formed a new mountain range. Again the mountains eroded, leaving a low flat plain with hills of tilted rock layers.

The tilt in rock layers along the canyon walls is evidence that sections of sedimentary rock were pushed up from below.

Hardened lava cascades below the butte called Vulcan's Throne at Toroweap Overlook where a volcanic cone once gushed molten lava.

The next 800 million years went by quietly, with no new strata being formed. Explorer John Wesley Powell called this long period the "Great Unconformity." A person standing by the Unconformity in the canyon wall can touch rock from 600 million years ago with one hand and rock from 1.7 billion years ago with the other.

Then, about 600 million years ago, things began to change on the planet. Living things began to multiply. A new geologic time period, the Paleozoic, meaning "old life," began.

Ten Layers of the Paleozoic

Most visitors to the Grand Canyon can pick out the ten colorful horizontal strata that formed above the tilted Grand Canyon Supergroup. These layers were laid down during the Cambrian Period, the first period of the Paleozoic Era, which extended from 570 million to 225 million years ago.

Again, seas formed in the region and then drained away, only to form again. Each change in the character of the region left its own stratum of rock, but this time things were different. The remains of newly evolved life were locked into the rock.

In the rocks of the earlier Precambrian Era, animal and plant fossils are hard to find and, when

The evening light on Deva, Brahma, and Zoroaster Temples *(left to right)* on the North Rim of the Grand Canyon accentuates the colors and shapes of the many rock layers in the buttes.

ROCK LAYERS OF THE GRAND CANYON WALLS

The Grand Canyon Supergroup is a group of rock layers laid down about 1.2 billion years ago. Consisting of eight layers of sedimentary rock, this group was probably covered with water, but not at all times.

Found above the Grand Canyon Supergroup is the Tapeats sandstone. This stratum is probably composed of the sands of beaches that edged the sea covering the region.

The next layer is the Bright Angel shale. Water covered this region, depositing mud, silt, and fine-grained sand to form the greenish Bright Angel shale layer containing fossils or trilobites—primitive crustaceans.

The mottled gray Muav limestone layer was deposited from limestone dissolved elsewhere and transported into these layers. The Muav limestone, Bright Angel shale, and Tapeats sandstone make up a group of shallow water and coastline layers called the Tonto Group.

Above the Tonto Group, shallow tidal flats formed along rivers and streams that crisscrossed the surface of the region. They left behind the purplish Temple Butte limestone stratum. The fossils of freshwater fish indicate that this water layer was locally non-marine. Sometime earlier, channels in the Muav limestone rocks filled with Temple Butte limestone.

The bright-red Redwall limestone stratum appears red but is actually composed of light gray limestone, the variety that formed under warm, shallow seas. The bright-red color comes from iron oxide that seeped onto the face of rock from the formation just above it, the Supai group. Redwall limestone holds many marine fossils, indicating that this region was covered with water. The water retreated before the Supai group was formed, leaving a limestone surface with a tropical environment.

Again, the sea moved in. But water didn't cover the entire area. Slow rivers and migrating shorelines deposited silt, clay, and sand that formed the next stratum, the Supai group. To the west of this coastal plain area is limestone that forms in seawater, indicating that the sea reached the western part of the Grand Canyon region during this period.

The deep-red Hermit shale layer, above the Supai group, formed from thick layers of mud deposited by rivers draining lands to the north and east. The canyon region was a floodplain during this period. There are many fossils in the shale.

The Coconino sandstone layer, known as "the bathtub ring," formed from pure quartz particles. The winds piled the sand into great dunes. Reptiles shared the territory with insects and scorpions that left their tracks in the sand. Then the seas came again. They left behind marine fossils and deposits making up the pale yellow and gray limestone of the Toroweap formation.

The light-colored cap or top layer on which you stand as you view the Grand Canyon is the Kaibab limestone stratum, also formed in seawater. The Kaibab deposits mark the end of the Paleozoic Era.

Kaibab Limestone

Toroweap Formation

Coconino Sandstone

Hermit Shale

Supai Group

Redwall Limestone

Temple Butte Limestone

Muav Limestone

Bright Angel Shale

Tapeats Sandstone

Tonto Group

Grand Canyon Supergroup

Colorado River

Vishnu Schist

Zoroaster Granite

Vishnu Schist

they are located, they show only invertebrate animals, such as jellyfish, and simple plants, such as marine algae and spores. But during the Paleozoic Era, new forms of life began to leave their traces in the rocks. Fossils from the Paleozoic Era indicate that fish, amphibians, reptiles, insects, and complex mosses and ferns were evolving.

Much of the limestone rock of these canyon layers was deposited by living organisms that secreted lime (calcium carbonate). However, limestone can be dissolved and moved elsewhere to form other kinds of "secondhand" limestone. Both new and "secondhand" limestone are present in the canyon.

In the middle of this sequence of layers, we see the remains of a period when the climate became increasingly dry, and the region became a desert. The rock-forming deposits of the Coconino sandstone were sands left as windblown sand dunes.

The Age of Reptiles

The Mesozoic Era, from 225 million to 65 million years ago, is known as the Age of Reptiles. During this "middle-life" era, the Grand Canyon region was covered by tropical forests and coastal swamps. Dinosaurs of many varieties roamed the land.

Rocks formed during the Age of Reptiles once covered the Grand Canyon region, but there are few traces of them now. All that remains of the sandstone and shale laid down during the Mesozoic Era are a few remnants such as Red Butte, Cedar Mountain, and the Vermilion Cliffs. The actual canyon had still not begun to form when the Mesozoic Era ended, but the entire Grand Canyon region was above sea level for much of that time.

The rocks layers of the Grand Canyon are full of exposed fossils. The picture below shows fossils of sea animals called crinoids imbedded in a slab of Kaibab limestone.

Up to the Present Day

The Cenozoic (or "recent-life") Era began 65 million years ago and continues today. During this era, the Grand Canyon itself was carved out of the rock formations laid down during the Paleozoic and Precambrian eras.

Widespread erosion wore away the Mesozoic Era deposits. Geologists estimate that 4,000 to 8,000 feet (1,220 to 2,440 m) of sandstone and shale were eroded, leaving the Paleozoic Era rocks uncovered. But new rock was also formed when magma rose to the surface. There it hardened into igneous rocks, the third category of rocks.

Volcanoes poured lava into the newly forming canyon at least ten times. The Colorado River was dammed in its flow—once by a 1,400-foot- (420-m-) high lava dam. A lake created by that dam backed up into the canyon a distance of 150 miles (240 km). The western Grand Canyon contains cinder cones, petrified lava flows, and basalt columns formed during this violent period. The last major eruption in the area was in A.D. 1064 near the San Francisco Peaks.

WHAT'S ON THE BUTTES?

From either rim, you can't miss the buttes, the flat-topped mountains that rise sharply from the floor of the canyon. They are mountains capped by flat layers of hard rock that has not yet eroded away. Some of the buttes are several thousand feet high.

Wondering what, if anything, lives on the buttes, biologists made a difficult expedition up to the top of the Shiva Temple butte in 1937. With much public interest and joking that living dinosaurs might reside there, the climbers reached the top. What they discovered in that seemingly inaccessible place were not dinosaurs but plenty of mule deer antlers, coyote tracks, and porcupine quills. The remains of rodents indicated that cougars and cacomistles (ringtail cats) had lived in the elevated area.

The climbers also discovered that ancient Native Americans called Anasazi had been there, perhaps 1,000 years ago. The "ancient ones" left many arrowheads, scrapers, drills, and piles of flint chips. The tools had been chipped out of chunks of rock, called chert, in the Kaibab limestone, the cap layer of the butte.

Chapter Five

Native Americans

F ive tribes of Native Americans presently occupy the Grand Canyon region. The plateaus surrounding the canyon are home to the Hopi, Navajo, Paiute, and Hualapai. The Havasupai are the only people who live in the Grand Canyon itself.

The Earliest Inhabitants

Animal figures made out of split twigs are the oldest evidence of human life within the Grand Canyon. The twig figures are pierced with tiny sticks that may represent spears. They were placed in isolated caves, where they were apparently symbols of religious rites held to ensure a good hunt.

The figures were fashioned by prehistoric hunter-gatherers who roamed the region about 4,000 years ago. Although the figures were discovered in the 1930s, they were not tested to determine their age until 1963 when a second group was found. A process called carbon dating placed their creation at about 2145 B.C. Similar twig figures have been found in southwestern Utah, southern Nevada, and southeastern California.

There are no signs that the makers of the split-twig figures lived in the canyon very long, and we have no idea what happened to them. It was another 1,400 years before other signs of human habitation were left.

"The Indians of the Grand Canyon country had lived in harmony with the land that supported them. They did little to change the face of nature. They were at one with the earth and could not easily survive under the impact of those who exploited it."
— C. Gregory Crampton in *Land of Living Rock,* 1985

The Anasazi people built boxlike buildings of stone and mud called pueblos, similar to the ones below.

Anasazi, the Ancient Ones

The next known occupants of the Grand Canyon are referred to as the Anasazi. The name means "ancient ones" and was given to the early people by the Navajo, who later moved to the region and found remains of the early culture.

The Anasazi, who were hunters and gatherers when they first moved into the canyon around A.D. 700, began to farm, adding corn to their diet. As corn production increased, they built more permanent settlements. They lived in pithouses, with rooms dug in the earth. However, by A.D. 800, small pueblos were built on the canyon rims and within the Grand Canyon itself. Tusayan Pueblo, an 800-year-old Anasazi ruin on the South Rim, dates to 1185.

By 1100, the Anasazi were growing crops on the floodplains along the river and in the side canyons. Warm temperatures within the canyon created a longer growing season than occurred up on the rim. The Anasazi occupied the canyon during the summer growing season and then moved to the rim where firewood was plentiful during the cold winter months. They wove elaborate baskets for use as cooking pots. Pueblos, storage granaries, and trails marked the canyon floor.

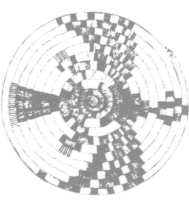

The Anasazi at Tusayan Pueblo wove very beautiful trays from which they served food.

By the thirteenth century, the Anasazi had disappeared from the Colorado Plateau. Although no one knows for certain why they left, hundreds of square miles must have been deforested for firewood and roof beams for their houses. A series of droughts in the entire Southwest, lasting more than a hundred years, further deforested the land. As the human population grew, the nutrients in the soil were used up. And perhaps they could not defend themselves against other tribes. Whatever the reasons, the Anazasi moved south and east, eventually becoming the Pueblo peoples of today.

The Anasazi of Tusayan Pueblo made several kinds of smooth, painted pottery.

But the apparent speed with which the Anasazi left the canyon remains a puzzle. So many tools and personal belongings were abandoned that some archeologists think the people expected to return the next season.

The Pai People

By the 1300s, the Coconino Plateau was occupied by the Cerbat or Pai people. The Pai were hunters and gatherers who learned to plant crops near permanent springs and in fertile lands within the canyon. They lived in rock shelters or sturdy domed houses, called wickiups, which were made of branches covered with juniper bark. The Pai traded with the Hopi and Paiute living north of the canyon. The Havasupai and the Hualapai, who occupy the western section of the South Rim, are descendants of the Pai.

In 1540, when Spanish explorers first visited the area, they were led by Hopi guides familiar with the canyon. The Hopi lived on the plateau farther east, as they do today. The Pai people hunted, gathered, and farmed on the South Rim. The Paiute hunted and foraged on the plateau north of the canyon.

Havasupai

The Havasupai—the People of the Blue-Green Water—are the only Native Americans now living in the Grand Canyon itself. The Supai, as they call themselves, have lived for centuries in Havasu Canyon, one of the most spectacular canyons in the system. It has dark-red sandstone walls, rich vegetation, blue-green waters, and sparkling waterfalls.

The people live around Havasu Creek, in a village 2,000 feet (600 m) below the rim where the canyon is only 0.25 miles (0.4 km) wide. The creek is a tributary of the Colorado River that reaches the main river over a series of waterfalls. The pools of the creek appear to be varying shades of green and blue, though a glass of creek water appears clear. The color is created by the reflection of the sky on sediments in the streambed and minerals dissolved in the water.

Steep trails connect the village with the plateaus where the Supai hunted deer and antelope and gathered pine nuts, seeds, and berries. During the long growing season, they raised corn, melons, beans, and squash in the canyon. Part of the crop was dried and stored in sealed caves in the cliff walls.

Havasu Creek flows toward the Colorado River through a series of rapids and waterfalls *(top)*. The water looks bluish-green in color *(left)*, but it is actually clear. Calcium carbonate dissolved in the water settles out to form hard travertine terraces. This mineral gives the water its color. The Havasupai people call themselves the People of the Blue-Green Water from the creek.

43

When mineral deposits were found and white men began to visit the canyon, a reservation for the people in the canyon was proposed. The Havasupai chief, Ko-hot, asked only for enough land to maintain the tribe's farming. The reservation set up in 1882 included just the tribe's summer home, which consisted of 518 acres (210 ha) on the canyon floor. The reservation was the smallest of all Indian reservations until 1975, when federal legislation expanded the reservation to include 185,000 acres (75,000 ha) on adjacent rims.

Today, these Native Americans farm only the 150 acres (61 ha) that are arable on the canyon floor. The approximately 700 members of the tribe live on welfare, government-surplus food, and fees from occasionally guiding tourists on horseback into the canyon. The people are malnourished, though public health efforts in their behalf have recently extended their life expectancy. Few of them speak English. One telephone serves the entire village, and pack trains bring mail three times a week. The development of the Grand Canyon as a major tourist destination has not improved their lives.

Today's Tribes Around the Canyon

Four other tribes of Native Americans live on the plateaus surrounding the canyon. The Navajo, who now occupy most of northeastern Arizona along the Painted Desert and to the edge of the Grand Canyon, did not enter the Four Corners region until the 1600s. They took over the large abandoned cliff dwellings left by the Anasazi. But they did not enter the canyon itself until the 1860s when they used it as a refuge from the U.S. Cavalry. The Navajo formed an alliance with the Paiute to push back the whites, but they finally agreed in 1870 to make peace with the settlers. The Navajo fared better than some tribes when their reservation size was established. By 1884, their reservation was 15 million acres (6.07 million ha), the largest in the country. Today, the people tend large flocks of sheep.

The Navajo tribe is the largest of all Native American groups in the United States. Known for their distinctive costumes, the Navajo live in the arid lands near the Grand Canyon.

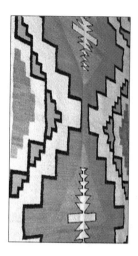

The Hopi live on a series of mesas, or raised, flat areas, 75 miles (120 km) east of the Grand Canyon, completely surrounded by the Navajo Reservation. Long familiar with the canyon, they may be descendants of the Anasazi. The Hopi were active traders. Hopi ruins, pots, and painted symbols are found in the canyon, and the salt deposits important to Hopi ceremonies are nearby. The ceremonies involve masked persons who represent the kachinas, ancestral spirits believed by the Hopi to directly influence the natural forces that bring rain and fertile crops.

The Paiute and the Ute, both Shoshone-speaking tribes, were moving into the Kaibab north of the canyon as the Anasazi were leaving. Individual Paiute were captured by the Ute tribe and sold into Mexican slavery in the early 1800s. Paiute territory was invaded by the advancing Navajo in the 1860s and by settlers in the 1870s.

When they could no longer live by hunting and gathering, the Paiute asked for a reservation. Two reservations were established—the Shivwits Reservation near Santa Clara, Utah, and the Kaibab Reservation, near Pipe Spring, Arizona. Their native life had almost disappeared by 1900 except for the Ghost Dance movement, which believes that a native messiah will restore their land.

The Hualapai, or People of the Pine Tree, are really one people with the Havasupai found down in Havasu Canyon. The two groups occupied most of the land south of the Grand Canyon. After the Hualapai War in the 1860s, the Hualapai were moved to the Colorado River Reservation, which was established near La Paz, Arizona, in 1865 for all the tribes in the Colorado River Basin. The reservation was crowded, and the people were expected to be farmers instead of hunters. They were used to open ranges and high plateaus, not a low and hot region. Many died. Others escaped and returned home to work in mines and on ranches or wander as nomads.

Aware that the coming of the railroad would only worsen their situation, the Hualapai requested their own reservation, asking for land no one else

A young Hopi child performs the Eagle Dance.

wanted on the Hualapai Plateau. The land was rocky and had little water or grass and no minerals. Only a small portion of the Hualapai Reservation, established in 1883, has arable land.

For all the Native Americans of the Grand Canyon region, the old ways are dying. With the increasing focus on tourism in the area, it is unlikely their cultural heritage will be revived, except perhaps as a showpiece for the visitors.

The Havasupai people have lived near Havasu Creek *(above)* in Havasu Canyon for 700 years. Today the tribe's 700 people live in small settlements in the canyon *(right)*.

Chapter Six

Wildlife

In February, up to 12 feet (3.6 m) of snow may cover the North Rim, while flowers bloom at the bottom of the canyon. That kind of contrast makes the Grand Canyon unique.

Living things in the canyon region have most of the characteristics that a person would ordinarily need to travel several thousand miles to find. Plants and animals can live only in those specific areas where climate, food, water, and protection meet the needs of each particular species. This grouping of animal and plant life was first proposed as the "zone theory" by Dr. C. Hart Merriam a hundred years ago. He divided the North American continent into seven principal life zones.

A person would need to travel 3,000 miles (4,800 km) from the tip of Florida past Hudson Bay in Canada to pass through all of Merriam's life zones. However, one can pass through four of the seven just by descending into the Grand Canyon, and through two more (leaving out only the tropical zone) by including the region around the canyon.

Today, Merriam's concept of "zone" has been replaced by the idea of "biotic community." A biotic community is an association of plants and animals

The golden columbine grows on rocky ledges and in the forests of the Grand Canyon.

47

that meet one another's basic needs. Animals pollinate flowers, scatter seeds, and loosen the soil as they burrow and deposit feces. Plants, in turn, release oxygen and produce carbohydrates that provide energy for animals.

The Grand Canyon is home to six different communities of plants and animals. Only a few feet in altitude can keep a living thing from migrating from one community to another, though sometimes plants and animals of one community may be found in another. And, of course, birds and many reptiles move freely among the different communities.

The biotic communities in and around the canyon include the river, or riparian, life; the desert scrub, which includes much of the canyon; the piñon-juniper community surrounding the entire canyon; the yellow pine and spruce-fir forest communities; and the mountain grassland, which is located in meadows within the spruce-fir forests. The following pages describe examples of the living things in these communities.

The blue spruce grows on the North Rim of the Grand Canyon and is part of the spruce-fir community.

Upsetting Nature's Balance

As in every ecosystem where humans have interfered, the big mammals of the canyon region have suffered. By 1910, for example, desert bighorn sheep, primarily inhabitants of the desert scrub, were on the verge of extinction in Arizona. Miners

Trophy hunters will pay guides from the Hualapai tribe up to $20,000 for the chance to kill a bighorn sheep.

shot them for food, livestock brought into the area gave them diseases, their waterways were choked off, and they were separated from each other by farms and highways.

Finally, desert bighorn sheep were found only in the Grand Canyon and on a few remote mountain ranges in southwest Arizona. Protective game preserves were established in Arizona, but the sheep outside the canyon were cut off from water during periods of drought. For more than 20 years, a group of volunteers has been building water reservoirs for the sheep. They built fences that deterred wild burros but not the bighorns. Burros could go to other areas for water, but timid sheep will not. The volunteers' efforts have paid off. Today, there are about 4,500 bighorn sheep living in Arizona.

Wild burros are now very rare in the Grand Canyon region. Humans have been their main predator.

Wild burros have just about disappeared from the region. Burros, native to northeast Africa, were brought to the United States by the Spanish. Used by prospectors and miners, the burros were turned loose when the miners left the Grand Canyon. Descendants of those early burros lived in both the riparian and desert scrub communities, where they caused extensive damage. The number and variety of plants declined as much as 50 percent in places where the burros grazed, thus increasing soil erosion. Prior to 1969, the Park Service killed many wild burros, but the policy was abandoned when the public strongly protested the killing. Most of the remaining burros have been captured and moved to other places.

Another mammal that has been affected by humans is the mule deer. Mule deer are found throughout the canyon communities but particularly within the yellow pine and spruce-fir forests. Game animals were protected in the Grand Canyon Game Reserve between 1906 and 1924, but, unfortunately, their predators, such as cougars, were not. During

those years, hunters killed huge numbers of cougars, and the 4,000 mule deer increased to more than 100,000. That was far more than the North Rim could support. Though an effort was made to move some of the mule deer to the South Rim, 90,000 deer died of starvation and disease in the following 16 years. Today, the mule deer population of 10,000 appears to be balanced with the environment.

Mule deer (left) are named for their large ears. When their natural predators were exterminated, their population ballooned. Today, most agree that the deer population is just about right for the habitat available.

Changes in the River

In recent years, Glen Canyon Dam and the twenty other dams along the Colorado River have altered the river environment that once met the needs of the eight species of native fish in the Colorado and the Grand Canyon. The building of Glen Canyon Dam stopped the regular seasonal variations in the flow of the river, reduced the amount of silt in the water, changed summer water temperatures from warm to cold, and eliminated the quiet water areas used as spawning grounds. As a result, three native species—the Colorado squawfish, humpback chub, and bonytail chub—are endangered and now protected by state or federal laws. They are no longer found within the Grand Canyon, except for a small remnant population of humpback chubs near the mouth of the Little Colorado River. A few very old razorback suckers are seen, but they are not reproducing and will likely be gone from the Grand Canyon by the end of the century.

The razorback sucker used to spawn in shallow quiet areas along the Colorado River. These areas were eliminated when the Glen Canyon Dam was built.

Twenty species of nonnative fish introduced into the river by man now occur in its waters, including cold-water species that could not live in the predam warm waters. Among the most abundant are rainbow trout, brown trout, and brook trout. Fishermen are delighted with the new fishing waters, but environmentalists prefer to protect native life forms.

Prior to the opening of Glen Canyon Dam in 1964, seasonal flooding of the Colorado River washed away vegetation along the riverbanks. Regulation of the river's flow has permitted new growth that provides nesting places for birds not formerly common in the area. Eleven new species of birds have been added since 1976 and endangered peregrine falcons now nest in the area. In one recent year, 58 pairs were counted in the Grand Canyon and 37 pairs in the river corridor. Waterfowl such as grebes, egrets, coots, rails, and gulls are also attracted to the new riparian vegetation.

Canyon and River as Barriers

More than 70 species of mammals live in the different biotic communities of the Grand Canyon. The canyon and the river have posed a barrier to movement of some animals from rim to rim. Nine species are found only on the South Rim. Of the eleven species that live only on the North Rim, four are absent from the south side because they don't have suitable habitats. The others have been unable to cross the canyon or the river.

As a barrier, the canyon played an important role in the evolution of two kinds of large squirrels. Both are dark gray in color with a maroon stripe down the back. The Kaibab squirrel, which lives in the pine forest of the North Rim and is found nowhere else in the world, has a black belly and a white plumelike tail. The Abert squirrel, which inhabits the pine forest of the South Rim, has a white belly and a grayish tail. It seems likely that when pine forests grew at lower elevations, the two species were one. Today, scientists disagree as to whether the Abert and Kaibab squirrels are separate species.

Peregrine falcons were once rare in the canyon, but their numbers are now increasing.

The threatened Kaibab squirrel lives on the North Rim of the Grand Canyon. It survives on a diet of ponderosa, or yellow, pine seeds and pine bark.

Also found on the North Rim are several species of mice and rats unique to that side of the canyon. Studies of the separate species have not yet shown why the two species have not crossed the canyon, interbred, and become one species again. Biologists do not know whether squirrels can get to the bottom of the canyon or cross the river once they get there.

The poisonous gila monster lives in the arid regions of the Grand Canyon. Feeding at night, it survives on eggs, birds, and small mammals.

Birds and Reptiles

More than 260 species of birds have been observed in the Grand Canyon National Park. More than 200 of these either nest in the park or visit it annually. Birds, unrestricted by the gulf of the canyon, can live on either rim. The birds within the canyon are primarily desert species. Birds can tolerate higher air temperatures than mammals and can fly to water.

Some 37 species of reptiles live in the region, in all the biotic communities. However, only seven species of amphibians are in the area, because they generally require more water than is available in the Grand Canyon.

Snakes and lizards are well suited to desert environments, though the midsummer heat in the canyon may be too much even for them. And reptiles cannot tolerate winter on the North Rim. To cope with these extremes of temperature, reptiles may limit their activity to cooler nights in summer and may hibernate during winter. Snakes, including three species of rattlesnakes, are less common than lizards and are not often seen.

The cliffs of the Grand Canyon provide perfect nesting habitat for ravens.

LIVING COMMUNITIES OF THE GRAND CANYON

Along the banks of the Colorado River, cottonwoods, horsetails, and several varieties of willows grow. However, tamarisk, a nonnative tree, is the most common plant. Introduced from the Mediterranean area in the early 1800s, tamarisk forces out native plants. Its deep roots consume available water before more shallow-rooted plants can reach it.

Riparian mammals include ringtail cats or cacomistles (known to befriend prospectors), spotted skunks, river otters, beavers, rock pocket mice, and long-tailed pocket mice.The canyon wren, large black raven, and great blue heron are common along the river. Reptiles, including the unique pink-colored Grand Canyon rattlesnake, are found along the banks.

Only 11 of the 700 species of freshwater fish native to North America are found in the Colorado River System. Eight of the eleven Colorado River species can be found only within the Grand Canyon, and only four of the eight appear stable—flannel mouth sucker, bluehead sucker, speckled dace, and a small population of humpback chub.

Away from the river, the main community is desert scrub, featuring the low-growing blackbrush plant. Desert scrub occurs in the Inner Gorge, on the Tonto Platform, and at other intermediate canyon levels. Other common plants include honey mesquite, Mormon tea, segolily, yucca, ocotillo, and barrel cactus. Desert scrub mammals include the desert bighorn sheep, wild burros, coyotes, ringtail cats, rock squirrels, black-tailed jackrabbits, cliff chipmunks, and several varieties of mice and ground squirrels.

Surrounding the entire canyon is the piñon-juniper community, named for the piñon (pronounced "pinyon") tree with its edible nuts and for the Utah juniper. These two evergreen trees are the most common in the community. The piñon was important to local Native Americans who used it to build their huts. Piñon pitch was used as glue, waterproofing for woven baskets, and dressing for wounds. Delicious piñon nuts were a primary food source. Other main plants include cliff rose, Mormon tea, broadleaf yucca, blackbrush, and rabbitbrush. Animals of the community are mule deer, desert cottontails, gray foxes, swallows, ravens, swifts, piñon jays, and scrub jays, as well as an occasional mountain lion.

The yellow pine community is forest, located between 7,000 and 8,200 feet (2,100 to 2,460 m) above sea level. The yellow pine is also called ponderosa pine. Also found in this forest community are Gambel's oak, locust, mountain mahogany, and blue elderberry. Animals of the community include the rare white-tailed Kaibab squirrel on the North Rim, striped skunks, deer, porcupines, ground squirrels, wood rats, cottontails, shrews, and chipmunks.

Ocotillo, a desert scrub plant (top); a porcupine of the yellow pine community (middle); piñon trees frame the canyon (right).

The spruce-fir forest community (formerly called Canadian forest) is found only on the North Rim. The conditions common to this community occur at elevations above 8,200 feet (2,460 m)—cold weather, heavy snowfall (120 inches or 300 cm on the average), and a short growing season. Local trees include blue spruce, Engelman spruce, Douglas fir, white fir, aspen, and mountain ash. Animals living in this forest include deer, elk, mountain lions, bobcats, red squirrels, porcupines, chipmunks, gophers, and wild turkeys.

Spotted throughout the spruce-fir community of the North Rim are several meadows. These open spaces make up the mountain grassland community. Wildlife in these meadows includes gophers, weasels, chipmunks, wild turkeys, voles, and mule deer.

Quaking aspens, golden in the autumn, line the meadows of the spruce-fir community. This scenery resembles that found above 8,000 feet (2,430 m) in the Rocky Mountains of Colorado.

Chapter Seven

"Thus Far and No Farther"

National parks are created to preserve natural wonderlands for the benefit and pleasure of everyone and keep them permanently safe and accessible. The Grand Canyon has survived, fairly intact, because, until about 25 years ago, the number of people who visited the canyon was limited. Also, the technology used by early developers had little impact on it.

In 1903 Theodore Roosevelt foresaw the demands that would be put on the Grand Canyon. He noted, "We have gotten past the stage, my fellow citizens, when we are to be pardoned if we treat any part of our country as something to be skinned for two or three years for the use of the present generation, whether it be the forest, the water, the scenery. . . . Don't let them skin this wonderful country, as they will try to do."

Today there is no question that dams, power plants, mining claims, and the millions of visitors to the region have left their mark on the canyon. These intrusions will destroy the canyon, unless something is done now.

Setting limits can prevent this "skinning" of the canyon, as Roosevelt called it. A writer for the Sierra Club put it this way: "Everyone everywhere has a stake in the Grand Canyon and a right to see it—or simply to think about it—in its natural condition. And the right extends to those yet unborn. By a stroke of geographical good fortune, Americans count the canyon in their territorial limits. But possession entails responsibility; we hold the Grand Canyon in trust for all humankind.

One of the ways history will judge our civilization is by examining our execution of this charge. "To set up a national park or a wilderness area is to establish a limit, to say 'thus far and no farther' to development."

"Leave it as it is. You cannot improve on it. . . . The ages have been at work on it, and man can only mar it. What you can do is to keep it for your children, your children's children, and all who come after you, as the one great sight which every [person] if he can travel at all should see."
— Theodore Roosevelt in 1903

President Teddy Roosevelt visited the canyon in 1903. Three years later he created the Grand Canyon Game Reserve.

Claiming the Natural Resources

One fact preventing the establishment of a limit is that today, within the Grand Canyon National Park and also on its borders, five mining claims, approved many decades ago by the federal government, are still producing valuable raw materials. In 1903, for example, Daniel Hogan staked a claim to a copper mine that proved worthless, but the claim passed into other hands, and in 1953 high-grade uranium ore was discovered. The National Forest Service had to issue a permit for uranium mining.

The Park Service's Mining and Minerals Branch reports that there are more than 2,000 mining claims in 130 parks. Many mines have been worked and then abandoned. Their tunnels and pit openings remain exposed, creating safety hazards for visitors and park staff. In addition, some of them are worked with hazardous chemicals that get into the soil and water. For environmentalists, both still-functioning and abandoned mines are cause for concern.

The "People of the Blue-Green Water" down in Havasu Canyon are suing the National Forest Service for giving companies permits to mine. The Energy Fuels Nuclear and Union Pacific companies own two mines that affect the Havasupai people. One of them, Canyon Mine, is located near Red Butte, a sacred site, where the Havasupai pray and perform sacred rites. The proposed site of Sage Mine is only 5 miles (8 km) from their home.

The U.S. Supreme Court refused to hear the tribe's complaint that their water supply will be

Red Butte is a sacred place for the Havasupai tribe. The silt is being threatened by mining claims. The Havasupai are fighting to save Red Butte by suing the National Forest Service.

contaminated by uranium mining. The companies offered the tribe both schools and education money. One member of the tribe said, "We said 'no.' This is our life that is at stake. This is the only place we have left. . . . The companies want to see us deteriorate, they want to see us die. But we are not going to give up no matter how hard it gets."

The environmental concerns of the Havasupai are mirrored by other tribes. The Kaibab Paiute rejected a proposal to build a hazardous waste incinerator on their reservation. One coal company wanted to take clean water from under the Hopi Reservation and mix it with crushed coal so that it could be piped from the mine in Arizona to a power plant in Nevada. The process would make the water useless. The Hopi rejected the idea.

Sometimes the interests of Native Americans are harmed by seemingly helpful proposals. Navajo in Utah have opposed a federal wilderness designation that would protect more Utah land. The proposal seems like a good thing, but no vehicles are allowed in wilderness areas, so the tribal people could not gather firewood to heat their homes or collect plants for medicines and ceremonies. Making decisions that please environmentalists, native peoples, and business interests is never easy.

The South Rim draws 90 percent of the park's visitors each year. It is open all year, but the North Rim is usually open only from mid-May to mid-November, depending on the weather.

Crowds at the Canyon

What about the claims of the owners of the park—the American citizens who wish to enjoy the canyon? Should they be kept away from their wilderness heritage?

In 1915, only 100,000 people visited the canyon. By 1966, the figure had risen to only half a million. But in 1992, five million visitors saw the canyon—40 percent of them from foreign countries.

There are merely 2,000 parking spaces for the 20,000 cars that will enter the South Rim by eight o'clock each morning. Motorists park on endangered plants on roadsides, sometimes a few feet away from grazing mule deer, and vehicle pollution adds to the haze over the canyon. In addition, trash and human waste pollute the very scenery people come to see.

Noise from motorboats and airplanes is another problem. For many years, small airplanes from cities in Arizona, Nevada, and Utah flew sightseers over the canyon, creating noise and pollution. That problem has been stopped by prohibiting planes from swooping down within the canyon walls or flying directly over the canyon. But how do you prevent people from using their freedom to run a powerboat upriver?

In public areas on the canyon rim, chattering tourists eagerly spill out of their buses in search of a restroom or a cold drink. They break the great silence that was a special part of the Grand Canyon experience for early visitors. Fortunately, if you take a short walk away from the crowds, you can still experience a taste of that stillness.

Beginning in 1987, small planes and helicopters were no longer allowed to fly low or dip into the Grand Canyon. To cut down on noise pollution, federal law requires planes to fly higher over the canyon.

Canyon Caretakers

The Grand Canyon has a number of loyal watchdogs. The Sierra Club and other environmental groups were successful in keeping dams out of the canyon, but they did not foresee the changes that would be wrought by a dam constructed upriver from the canyon. They are now highly sensitive to the fact that all matters concerning the region are interconnected.

The Grand Canyon Trust is an organization that works to protect the Colorado Plateau through negotiation and lawsuits, education, and lobbying. Executive Vice-President Jim Ruch writes: "The problem is that the cost of conservation has never been figured into the price of things that started out as 'free goods'—soil, water, air, wildlife."

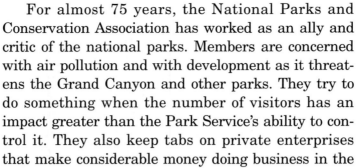

Over 22,000 visitors run the Colorado River on rafts each year. The Park Service closed Redwall Cavern in Marble Canyon to overnight camping because it was being destroyed by overuse.

For almost 75 years, the National Parks and Conservation Association has worked as an ally and critic of the national parks. Members are concerned with air pollution and with development as it threatens the Grand Canyon and other parks. They try to do something when the number of visitors has an impact greater than the Park Service's ability to control it. They also keep tabs on private enterprises that make considerable money doing business in the parks but pay only a small portion of their profits to the government.

In *Grand Canyon: Today and All Its Yesterdays,* Joseph Wood Krutch wrote in 1958: "The wilderness area, the protected nature reserve, and the recreation resort are different things: the first is for the smallest minority— that which is physically and psychologically up to the strenuousness of really primitive living. The second is for the larger minority which is interested in wild animals, in plant life, and in natural scenery, even though unprepared for life in a real wilderness. The third, of course, is for the majority whose tastes are not essentially different from those who frequent commercial resorts."

The North Rim is better protected than the South Rim simply because it is more difficult to get there. Most tourists will not go where the condition of the roads make automobile and bus travel uncomfortable. Keeping many back roads unpaved will keep some of the wilderness secluded.

Do we know enough about wildlife and vegetation to alter the delicate balance of nature? The sagas of the mule deer, the wild burro, and the tamarisk tree all say, "Hands off." What about "native versus non-native" species in any given spot? The truth is, we do not know if it matters to the survival of a region what species of fish we stock in a river.

A comprehensive river management plan that includes concern for the natural environment of the river, including the Grand Canyon and all other natural wonders along the length of the Colorado, should guide future decisions. Such a plan already exists for the Northwest and the Columbia River.

The Grand Canyon and the Colorado River have been entrusted to us. In the more than 90 years since Theodore Roosevelt voiced his warning about not skinning this wonderful country, we have learned much. We need now to act upon the knowledge.

Hiking in the Grand Canyon is increasingly popular, but visitors need to remember to stay on marked trails.

The Gifts of the Canyon

The most obvious gifts offered by the Grand Canyon are solitude and perspective—the reminder that something uniquely grand and complicated can develop in nature without human help. Such a place restores us to our proper position in the scheme of things. It helps us remember that we are part of a web of life, in which each species depends on the presence of every other species. We begin to expand the framework out of which we make decisions. We are renewed and, indeed, more peaceful, after viewing the splendor of the canyon.

Does that matter? There is little doubt that we are all part of a global community. As the world becomes more crowded, we need to bring our most peaceful, clearest-thinking selves to the business of living together. The entire Earth—and beyond—are "humankind's biotic community." The careful keeping of breathing spaces such as the Grand Canyon is vital to a future that can be lived with quality and grace.

Wotan's Throne as seen from Cape Royal reminds visitors of the irreplaceable majesty and solitude of the Grand Canyon.

GLOSSARY

arable – fit for plowing.

arid – lacking enough rainfall to support agriculture; for example, conditions in a desert.

biotic community – plants and animals that depend on each other in a specific, beneficial environment.

butte – flat-topped hill with steep sides; a small mesa.

era – a period of time; one of five major divisions of geologic time.

erosion – wearing away by the action of water, wind, or ice.

fossil – preserved impression, remains, or trace of an animal or plant from a past geologic age.

floodplain – land along a river that regularly floods.

generator – apparatus that makes electricity from the turning motion of a bladed mechanism called a turbine.

granary – storehouse for threshed grain.

headwater – the source of a stream.

hydroelectric power – electric energy made by the motion of falling water turning the blades of a turbine in a generator, usually within a dam.

igneous – formed by solidification of magma; one of three categories of rocks.

intrusive – formed by magma or molten rock pushing into or between other rock formations.

lava – molten rock that emerges from a volcano or from a fissure in the Earth's surface.

lichen – a plant combining algae and fungi.

magma – molten rock material within the Earth.

metamorphic – produced by a change in the composition of something, for example, when pressure, heat, or water changes the character of a rock; one of the three categories of rocks.

molten – liquefied by heat.

pueblo – a series of cliff dwellings; "apartment" houses dug out of cliff sides.

riparian – related to a river or other body of water.

sediment – matter that settles to the bottom of a liquid; material deposited by water, wind, or glaciers.

sedimentary – formed out of sediment; one of the three categories of rocks.

silt – loose sedimentary particles, less than .024 inches (0.625 mm) in diameter.

stratum – a layer or sheetlike mass of earth or rock of one kind lying between beds of other kinds. Plural: strata.

talus – rock debris at the base of a cliff or a slope, such as along the bank of a river.

transport – the process of transferring or carrying something from one place to another; to transfer or carry something.

upwarp – thrust upward toward a higher level.

weathering – chemical or physical breakdown of solid material, often by such weather elements as wind, rain, snow, and ice.

FOR MORE INFORMATION

Books

Babbitt, Bruce. *Grand Canyon*. Flagstaff, Ariz.: Northland Press, 1978.

Braun, Ernest. *Grand Canyon of the Living Colorado*. New York: Sierra Club-Ballantine Books, 1970.

Collier, Michael. *An Introduction to Grand Canyon Geology*. Grand Canyon, Ariz.: Grand Canyon, Natural History Association, 1980.

Fletcher, Colin. *The Man Who Walked Through Time*. New York: Vintage Books, 1967.

Foster, Lynne. *Exploring the Grand Canyon: Adventures of Yesterday and Today*. Grand Canyon, Ariz.: Grand Canyon Natural History Association, 1990.

Krutch, Joseph Wood. *Grand Canyon, Today and All Its Yesterdays*. Tucson, Ariz.: University of Arizona, 1958.

Loving, Nancy J. *Along the Rim*. Grand Canyon, Ariz.: Grand Canyon Natural History Association, 1981.

Walter, Steven L. *Grand Canyon, A Natural Wonder of the World*. Flagstaff, Ariz.: Camelback/Canyonlands Venture, 1991.

Whitney, Stephen. *A Field Guide to the Grand Canyon*. New York: Quill, 1982.

Videos

Grand Canyon. Reader's Digest, International Video Network.

Grand Canyon National Park. Bryce/Zion National Parks series, Wilderness Video.

Grand Canyon National Park. Rand McNally Videotrip Travel Guide, Video Cassette Recordings.

INDEX